INTRODUCTION

Welcome to the pages of bargain Backgrounds and Krazy Caleidoscopes. Be prepared for hours of coloring with many hypnotic patterns and mesmerizing kaleidoscopic imagery. I recommend putting on some good tunes and drift out of reality while coloring this myriad of images. Well, I don't want to keep you from coloring so get to it. Enjoy!

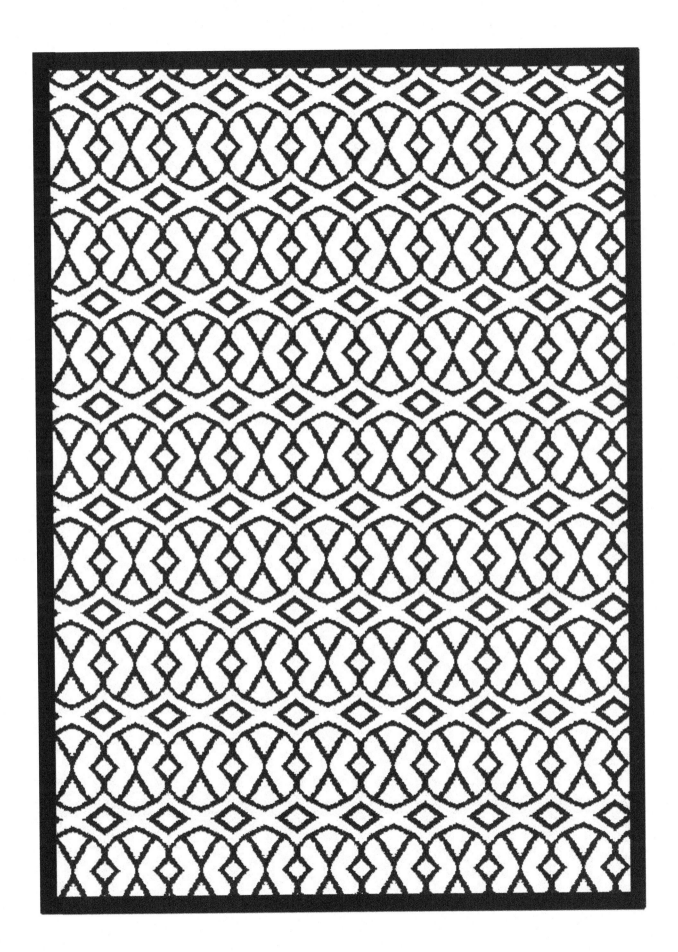

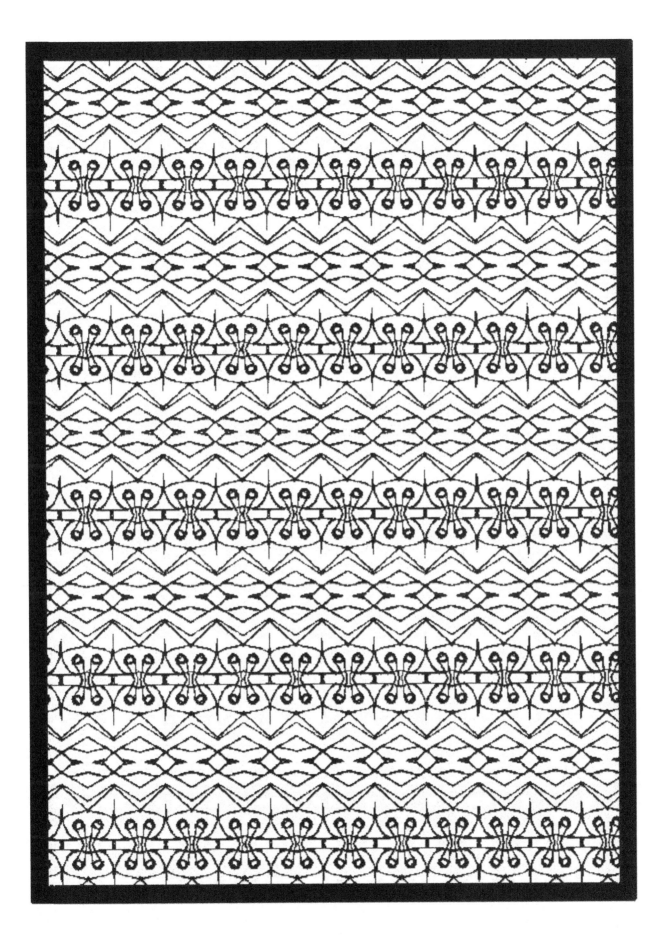

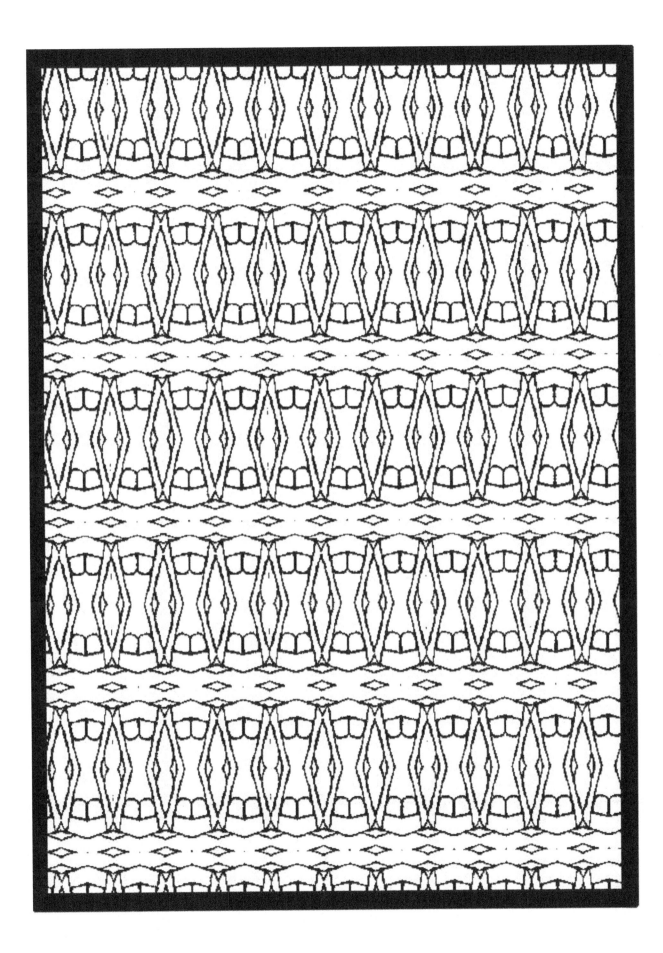

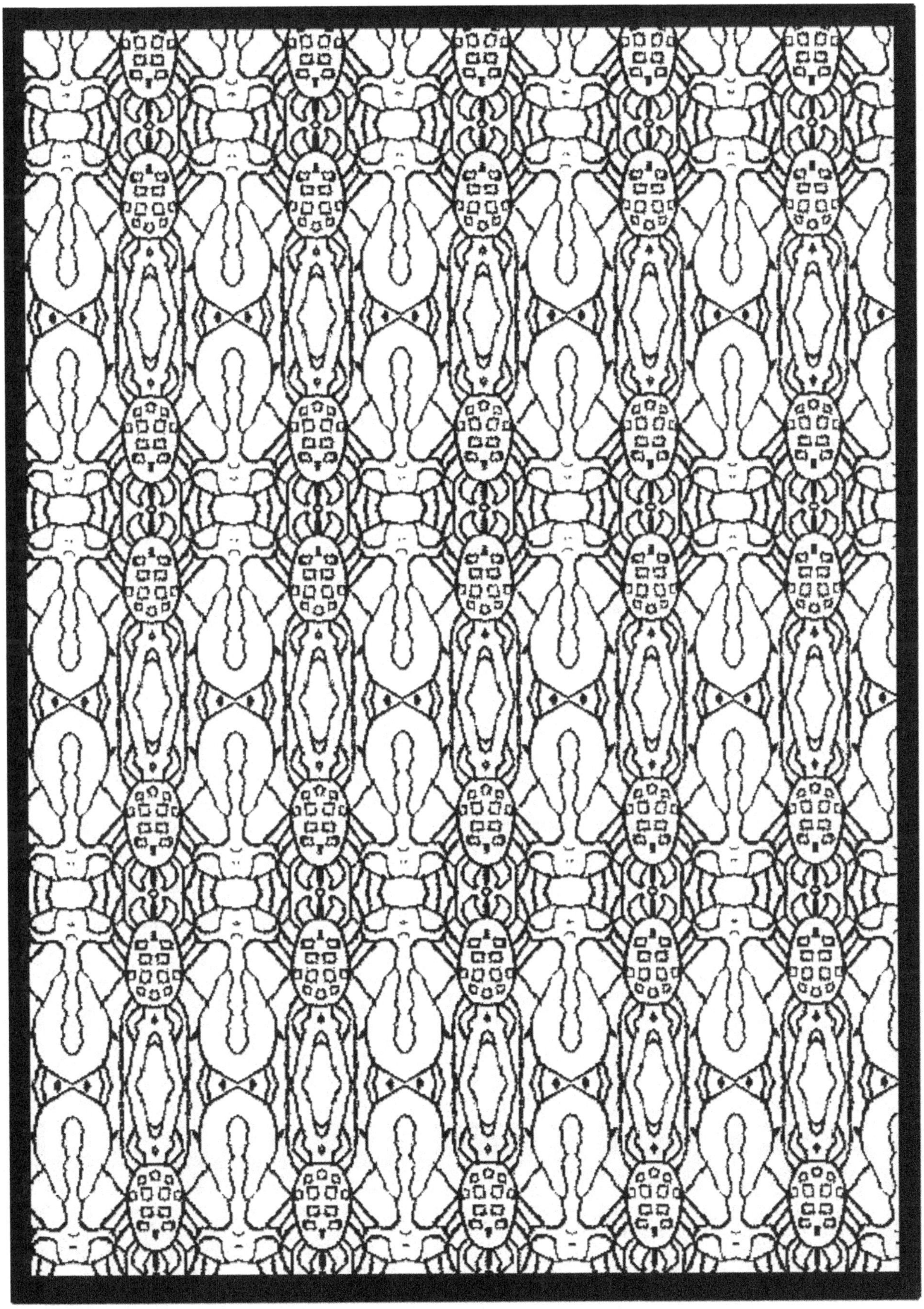

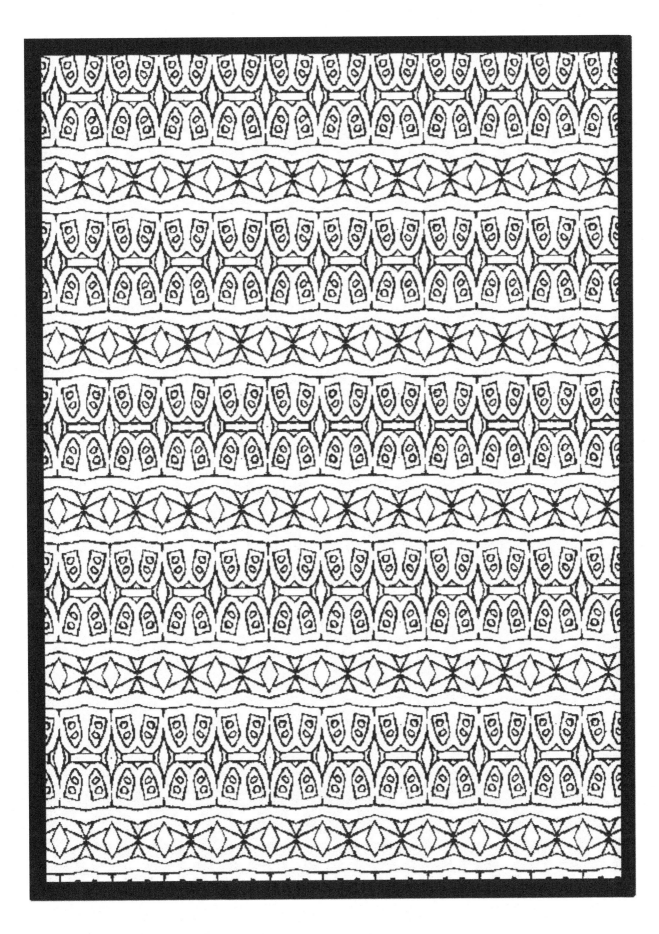

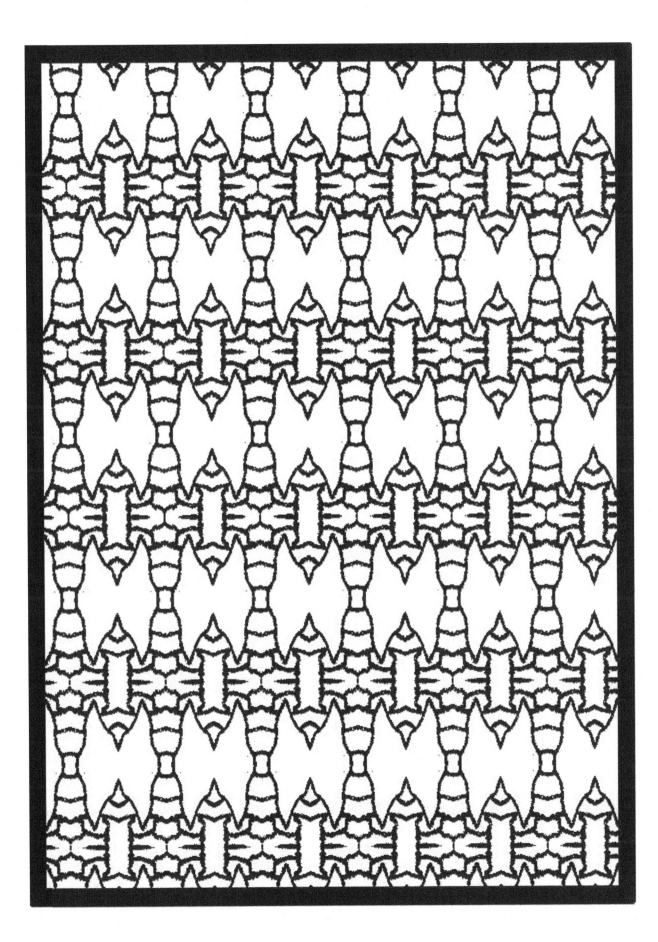

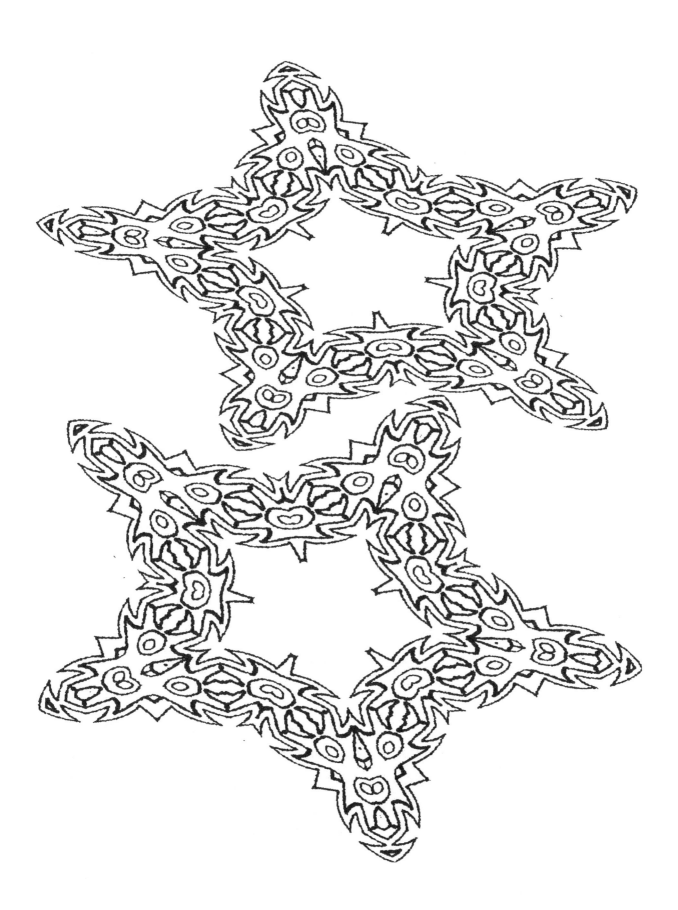

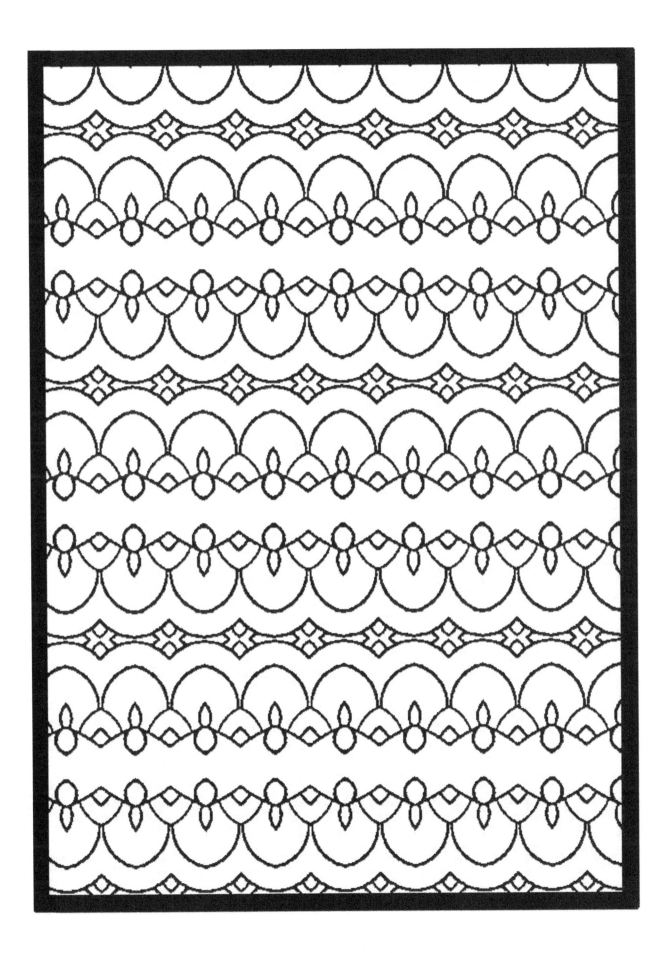

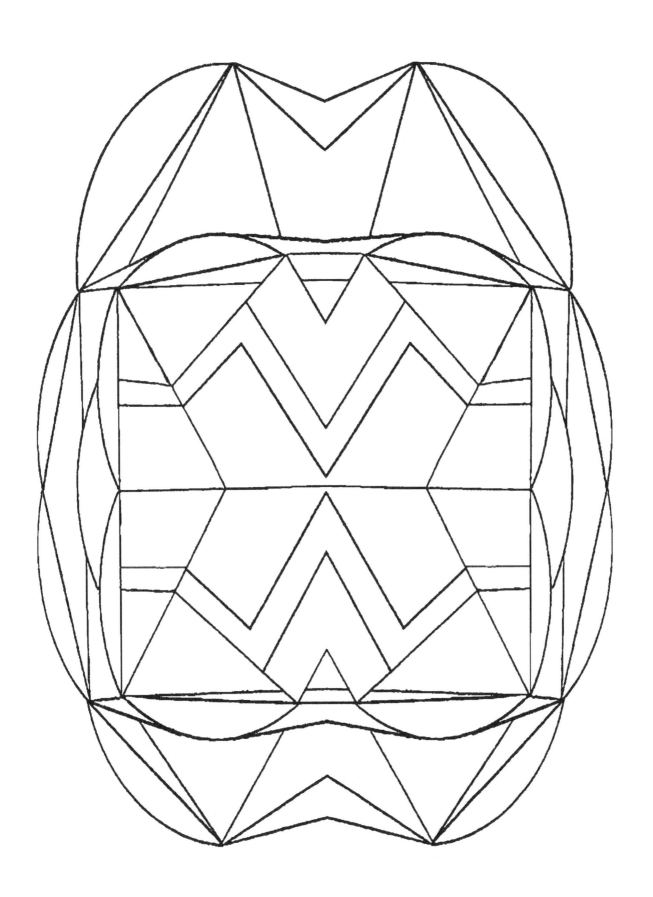

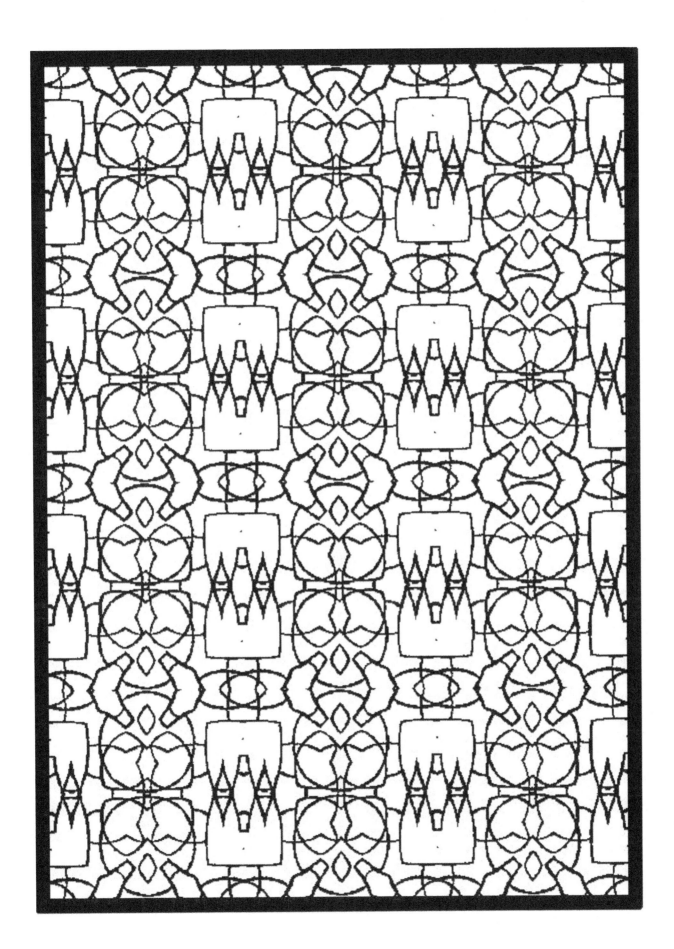

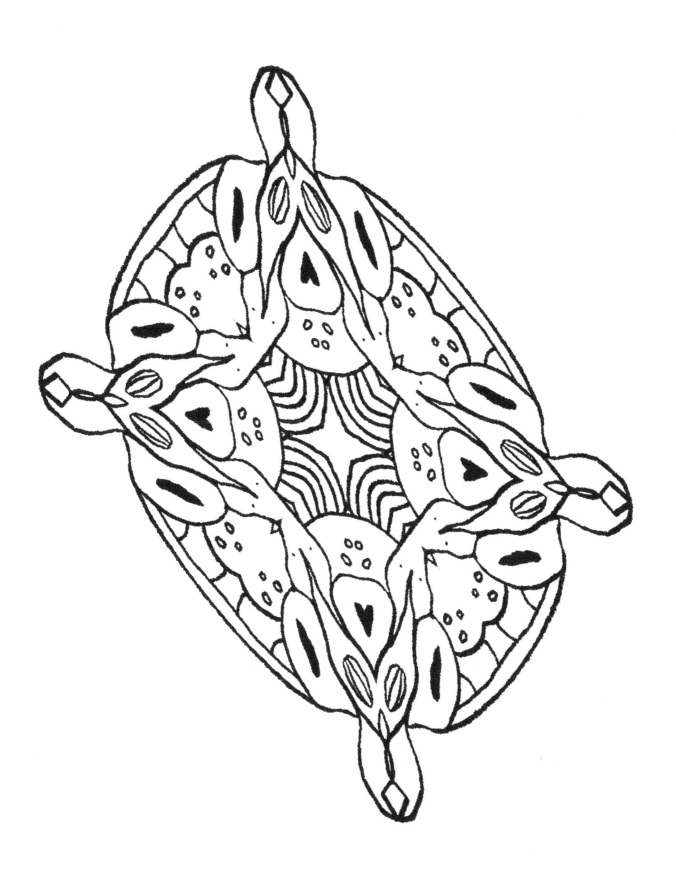

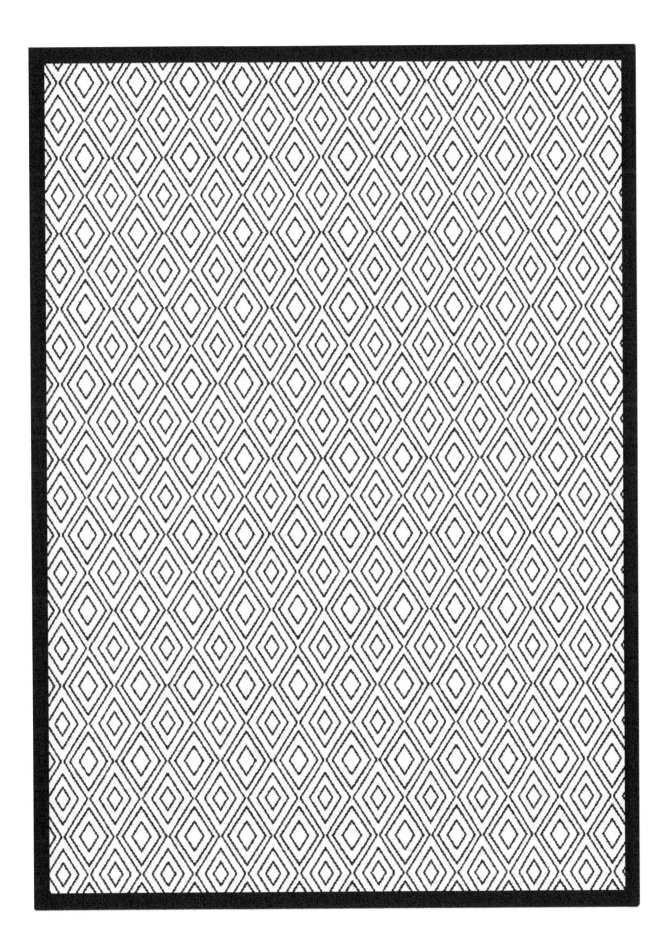

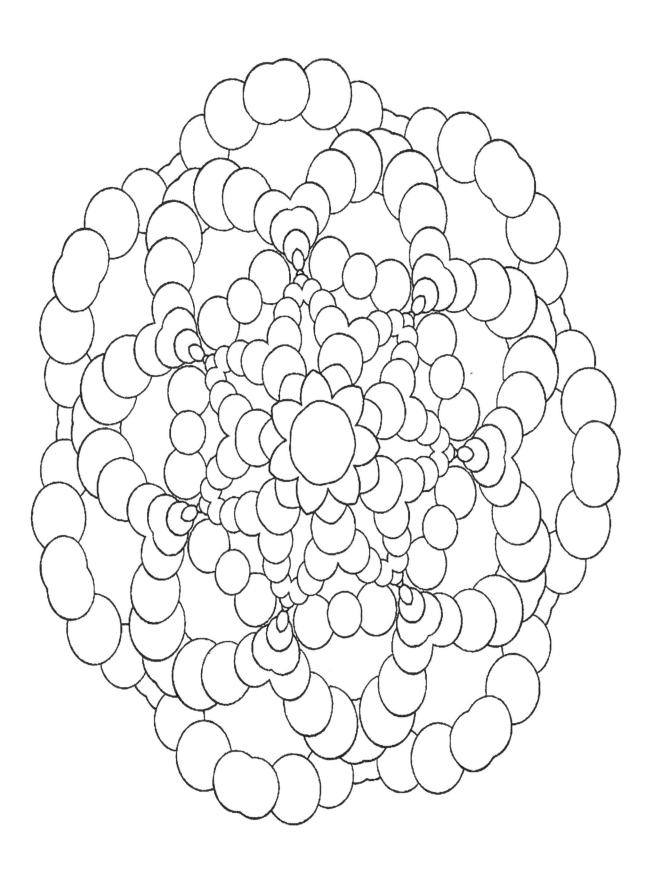

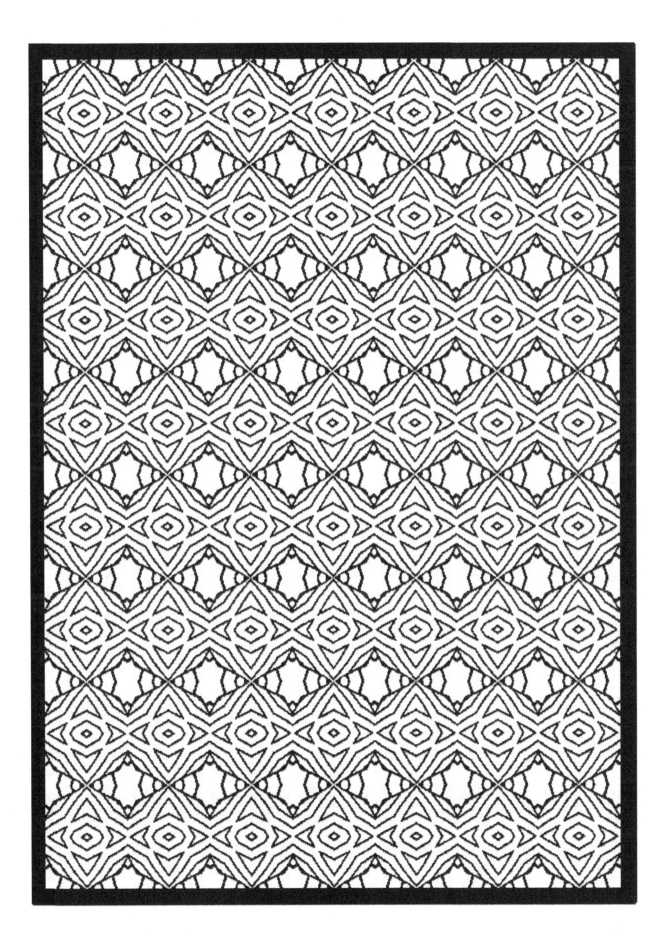

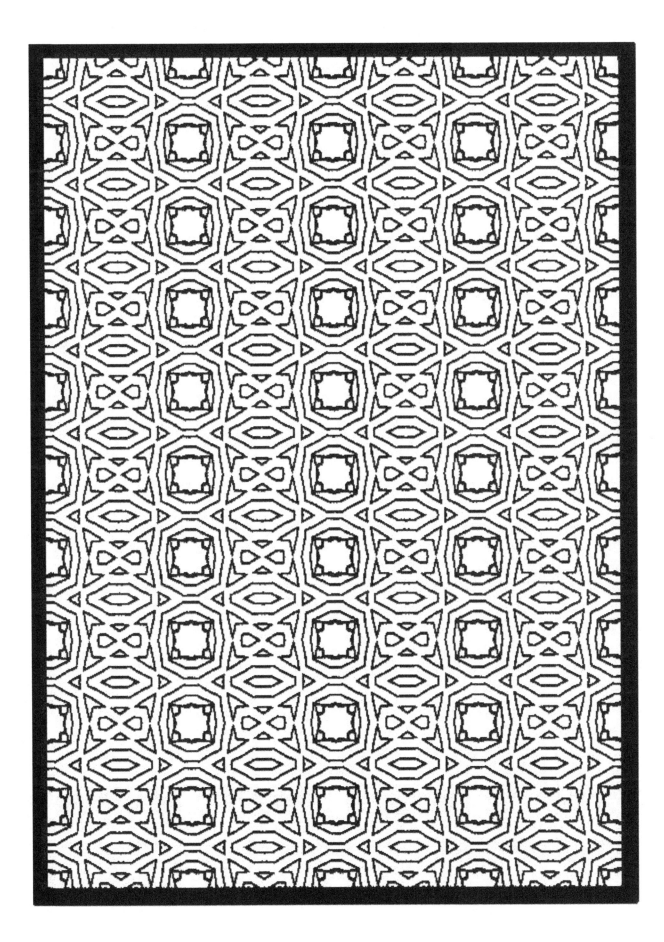

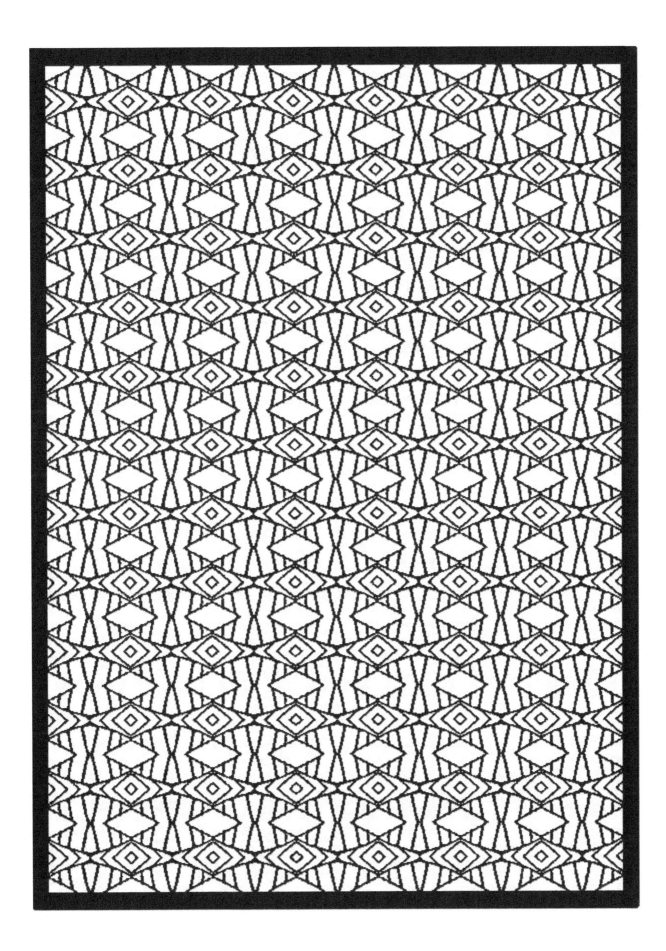

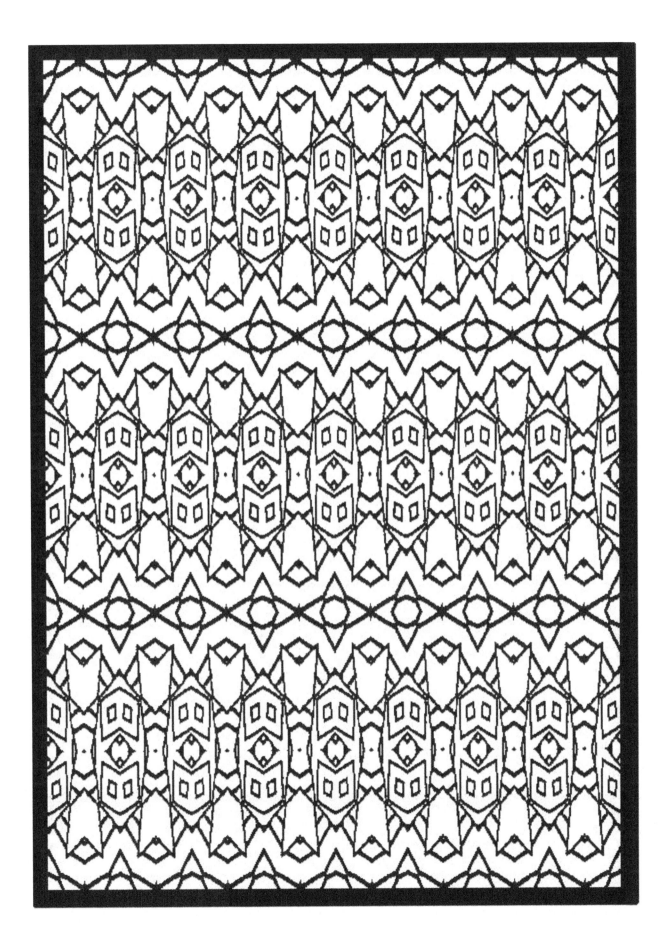

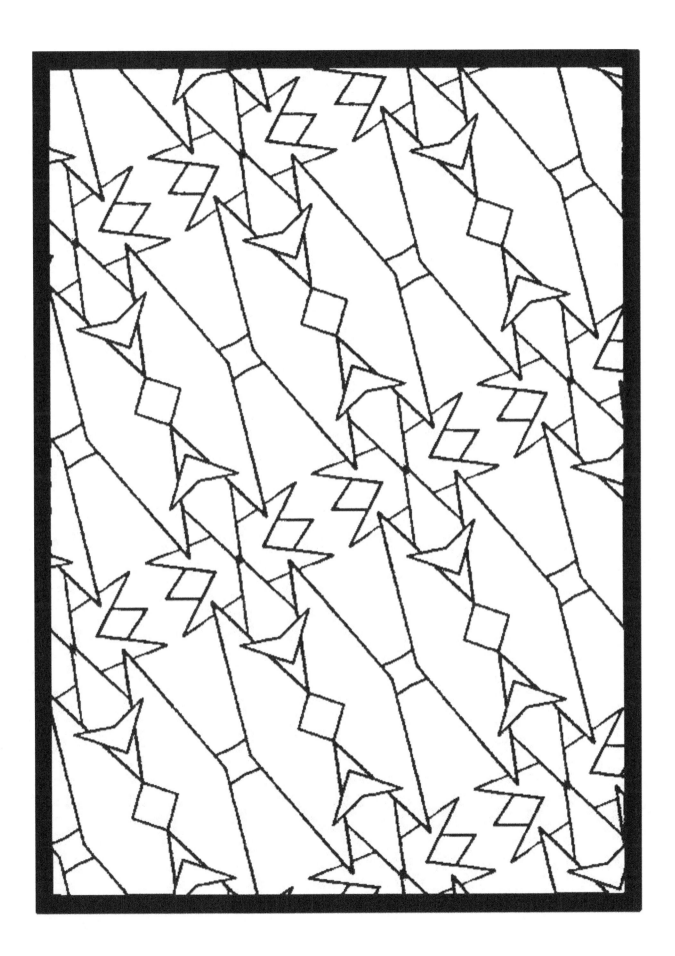

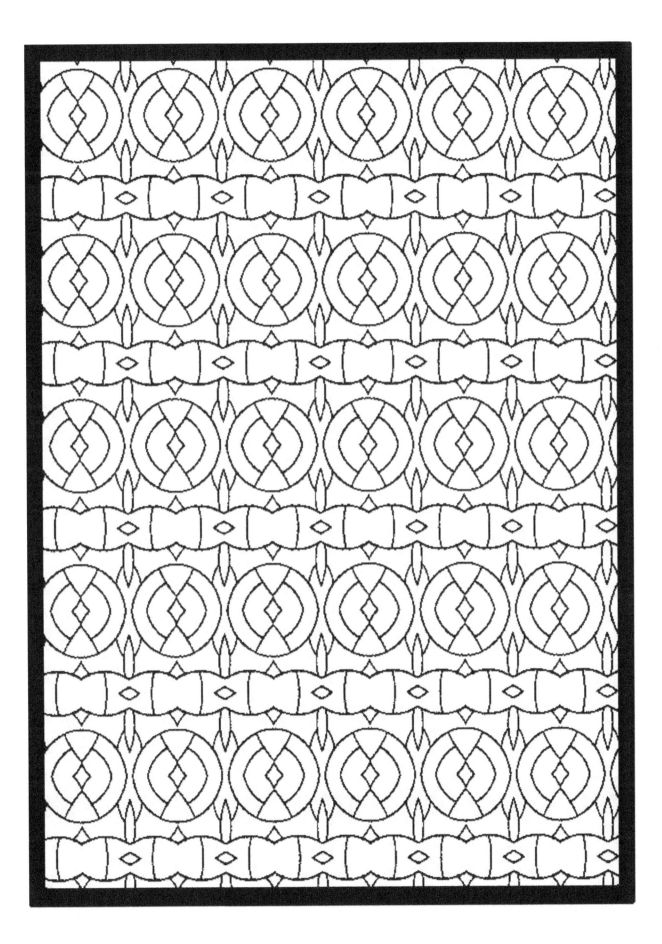

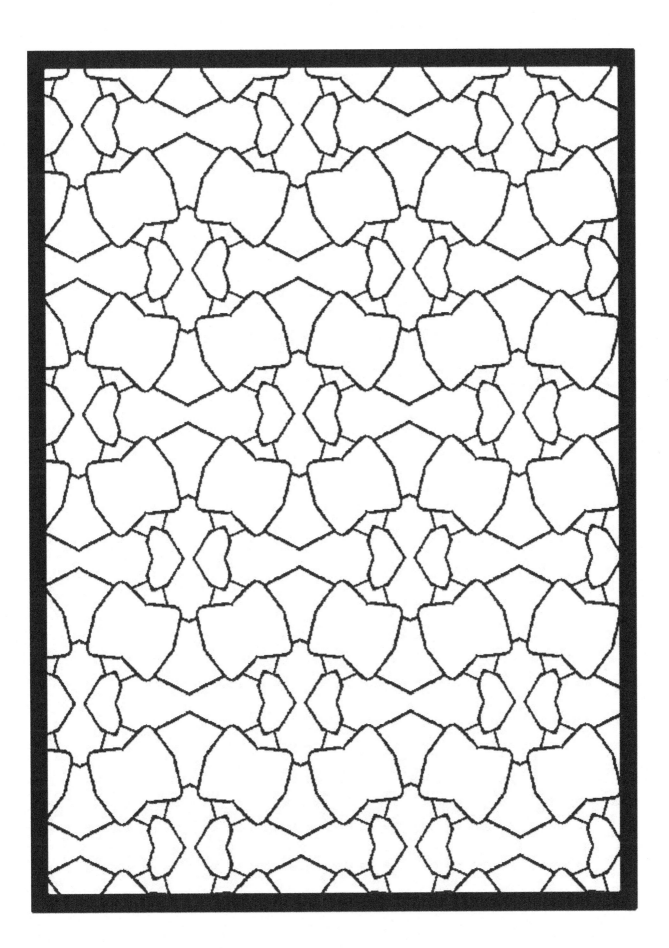

Special Thanks:

I just want to take a minute to thank everyone who has enjoyed my work and inspired me. There are so many people but the most notable are all my good friends, Ian, Brandon, Jeff, Lexi, Jade, Brandon, Jimmy, Dom, Nick, Melissa, and a bunch more. My parents for actually being happy for what I'm doing. You all are amazing. I love you and you're all the best. A special shout out to Michaela. I'm so happy for you and thanks for inspiring me to finally start getting on better myself and chasing my dreams. It's good to see you are doing well. Keep it up!

As always a special thanks to all of my grandparents watching over me. I love and miss you all so much. I try to live my life the best I can and through all of the lessons you each taught me. Thank you so much.

Made in the USA
Monee, IL
30 December 2020